IMAGES
of America
WESTERLY

IMAGES
of America

WESTERLY

Kathleen M. Fink and Courtland Loomis

ARCADIA
PUBLISHING

Published by Arcadia Publishing
Charleston, South Carolina

Library of Congress Catalog Card Number: 2004108959

For all general information contact Arcadia Publishing at:
Telephone 843-853-2070
Fax 843-853-0044
E-mail sales@arcadiapublishing.com
For customer service and orders:
Toll-Free 1-888-313-2665

Visit us on the Internet at www.arcadiapublishing.com

Contents

Introduction

Westerly is steeped in tradition, and its roots can be traced back over 250 years. In 1642 Mary Lawton and John Babcock, the first white settlers in the region, arrived on the east bank of the Pawcatuck River after fleeing from her family's opposition to their marriage. They got along very well with the Native Americans in the area and their son James was the first white child born in Westerly. Others from Newport began to arrive in 1664 and shortly thereafter their place on the river, Misquamicut, was incorporated as Westerly by the Colony of Rhode Island. It was one of the first towns under the Colonial Charter in 1663 and the fifth in the colony.

Westerly has flourished from that time onward, and there have been a myriad of changes in its industry, transportation, and pace of life. The fishing industry, granite quarries, and textile mills have all been important elements of life in Westerly. Approximately 80% of all Civil War monuments are made of Westerly granite, as are other monuments throughout the United States and the world. Modes of transportation have changed dramatically through the years: the sailing vessels, horses, and carriages of the mid-1800s were replaced by the open trolley cars of the late 1800s, which were in turn replaced by the autos of the early to mid-1900s. Popular fashions have changed as well, as is evident in the photographs of schoolchildren, sporting groups, fraternity and social gatherings, and individual portraits.

Despite the multitude of changes, many of yesterday's buildings can still be seen in Westerly today, and people still hold on to the traditions that were set down in early times by their forefathers. Westerly is full of proud people, who are appreciative of their roots—and justly so.

Kathy Fink
September 1995

Special thanks to Courtland Loomis for his help with the compiling of this book. Thanks also to Melinda Fink Tyler and Jim Curry for their hospitality, love, and encouragement.

One

Old Westerly

A trolley passes by the Briggs Building on Main Street in Westerly.

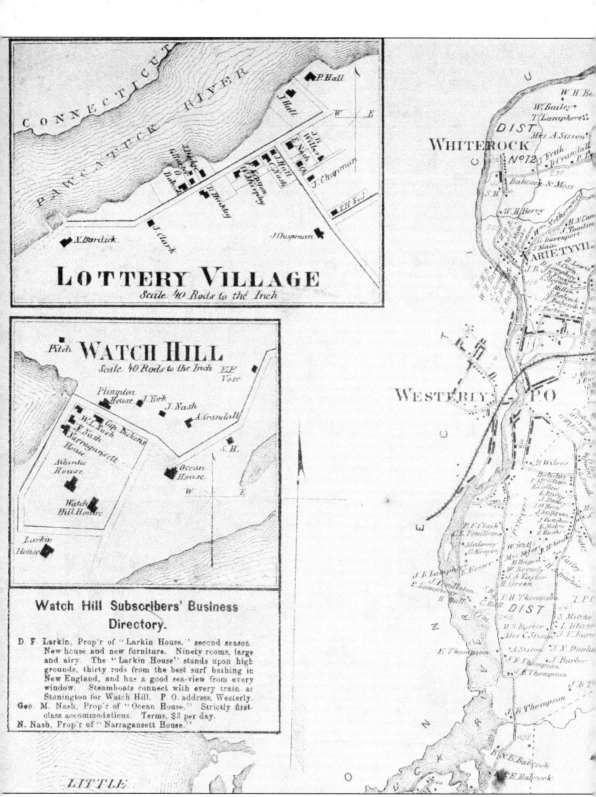

An 1871 map of Westerly.

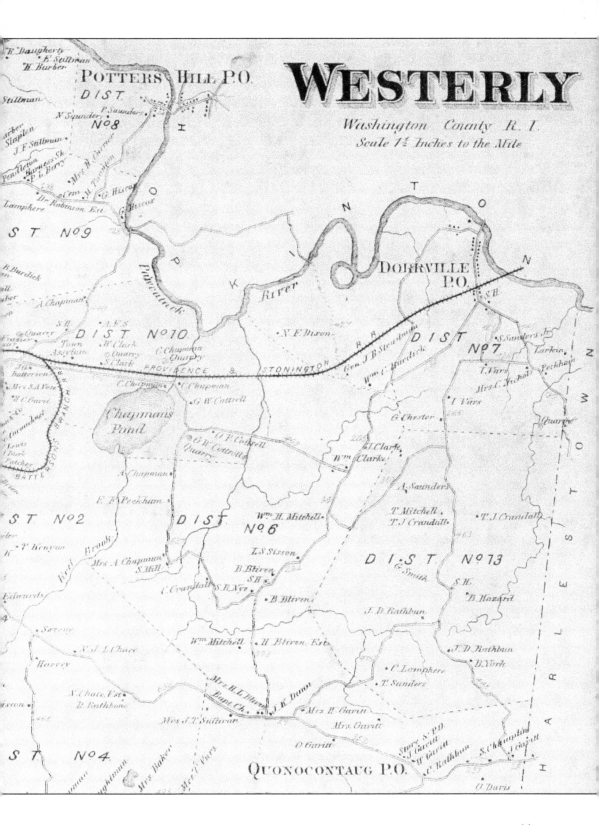

POTTERS HILL P.O.

WESTERLY

Washington County R.I.
Scale 1¼ Inches to the Mile

DIST N°8

DIST N°9

DORRVILLE P.O.

DIST N°10

DIST N°7

Chapmans Pond

Providence & Stonington R.R.

ST N°2

DIST N°6

DIST N°13

ST N°4

QUONOCONTAUG P.O.

A covered carriage moves around a parked cart in this view of Main Street. Could it be headed for the nearby livery stable? (WS)

The Westerly Public Library, from a postcard marked 1927.

This postcard, marked 1917, shows the new town hall and court house.

This photograph shows the old town hall following the Union Street fire in which the old fire station burned to the ground. (WPL)

A gentleman, who reminds one of Abe Lincoln, and a lady survey Dixon Square from their balcony above the post office in 1853. (GHU)

A woman strolls along Dixon Square as the girl with her glances in shop windows. (ENB)

A little boy appears sandwiched between two women as they walk through Dixon Square in 1934. One wonders if they are shielding his view of the signboard advertising ice cream and candy at the nearby store. (GHU)

Strollers in dresses and hats of the day pass by a working man, who seems to be the only person headed in the opposite direction. (GHU)

Three women walk down the sidewalk seemingly unaware that they may have caught the eye of the man in the background; or perhaps they are aware, as the woman in the middle seems to be saying something to the woman on her right and smiling. (GHU)

A little miss goes strolling in 1934. Could the gentleman be leading the way? (GHU)

A postcard view of the old town hall and fire station. The fire station was later destroyed by fire.

A man rests his feet on a nearby fence as he good-naturedly smiles for the camera. (WS)

Four men serenade with instruments of the time. (WS)

This trolley has just made the bend in Dixon House Square.

Two young boys sit at a curb in front of Fisher's Dry Goods Store and watch the world pass by on High Street in 1934. It is doubted whether they observed the "fifteen minute stop" sign. One of the boys is thought to be Pucki Priore. (GHU)

This postcard, marked 1921, shows High Street.

A view of High Street from the Dixon House around 1906.

High Street in Westerly, from a postcard marked 1912.

A view of High Street from Dixon House Square, from a postcard posted in 1914.

The junction of High and Broad Streets, from a postcard marked April 1914.

Two women in their finery take a buggy ride down Broad Street. The lady on the right seems to be contemplating a leap from the carriage, or perhaps she is hanging on so as not to fall. (GHU)

This photograph shows the remains of the buildings following the Star Theatre fire on West Broad Street in January 1913. (WPL)

The remains of the Dixon House (aka the Rhode Island Hotel) on Broad Street on April 16, 1928, following the fire which destroyed it. (WPL)

The young lad in the foreground seems to have forgotten the excitement of a fire on High Street on August 8, 1891, now that he has noticed the photographer and pauses long enough to smile. Notice the steam pumper, which drew water from an underground cistern to fight fires. During this fire the America Hall Block was destroyed. (GHU)

24

Majestic trees shade the Broad Street entrance to Wilcox Park.

This postcard shows a lovely gazebo and rustic steps in Wilcox Park.

A serene photograph of Wilcox Park.

The Westerly Brass Band poses in Wilcox Park. (WPL)

These people
are out for a
horse cart ride.

Lovely large trees compete for attention with telephone poles, trolley wires, and tracks in this photograph.

Trolley tracks make their way past these lovely homes in Westerly.

N. Y., N. H. & H. Depot, Westerly, R. I.

This postcard, marked 1913, shows the New York, New Haven, and Hartford Depot in Westerly.

Christ's Church, from a postcard marked April 1911.

A postcard view of the First Baptist Church.

The steeple and cross of the Episcopal church stretch above the trees.

This Stiles photograph shows the Grace Methodist Church on Grove Avenue. (WS)

This photograph of the Pawcatuck River was taken from Greenman Avenue across Margin Street.

Stately trees shade Margin Street as it curves along the Pawcatuck River.

31

A view of the Lorraine Mill on the Connecticut shore of the Pawcatuck River, and the pontoon bridge used to assist workmen who lived on the Westerly bank.

A view of the Pawcatuck River, which separates Pawcatuck, Connecticut, from Westerly.

Two

Photo Gallery

Mary Starr Utter with her doll and carriage at 106 High Street in 1897. (WS)

The Dunn family in the late 1800s. (GHU)

Mary Starr Utter riding "Dapple Gray" in 1897. (GHU)

Molly D. Utter relaxes in the parlor of the G.B. Utter I home. (WS)

A flashlight aided in the taking of this January 1898 photograph of Wilfred Brown Utter as he sleeps in a parlor chair. (WS)

Four cousins pose in their Sunday best. (WS)

Henry Utter gets a birds-eye view from his comfortable perch on the roof of a High Street house. (WS)

These four girls posed near a fence for the photographer. (GHU)

This portrait was taken at the home of Mrs. G.B. Utter. (GHU)

Ben Utter, Mary Starr Utter, and Henry Utter in the back yard of 106 High Street in the summer of 1892. (GHU)

Wilfred Utter was caught bathing in this 1895 picture. (GHU)

Will Stillman is shown here standing outside the Westerly Public Library in 1897. (WS)

Annie Allen and Julia McCarthy at 104 High Street in February 1897. (GHU)

Esther Myers, shown here at age sixty-six. On the back of the photograph it is noted: "Her appearance was such as to draw complete attention, bent over, hobbling along with the aid of a cane, talking to herself, she reminded one of the descriptions of the Salem women who were burned to death as witches." Ironically, she did end up burning to death when her two-century-old homestead burned on December 16, 1898. (WPL)

Sitting on a rock wall are Mary Starr Utter, Ruth Burdick, and Helen Wells Rogers in February 1898. (GHU)

George B. Utter with his customary bike, wearing his MVC (high school fraternity) hat in 1898. (GHU)

Wilfred and Mary Starr Utter in
1898. (GHU)

This April 8, 1899 portrait shows
Edward Babcock (1819–1908). He
was once the president of the Phenix
(?) Bank. His wife once donated the
corner of Elm and Broad Streets to
the Christ Church just before the
Civil War so that they could build a
larger church of granite. (WPL)

Six gentlemen pose for a portrait. From left to right are: (front row) William Hoxsie, Edward Francis Vose, and James Albert Brown; (back row) George Gavitt Stillman, Azro Norton Lewis, and William Howard Robinson. (WPL)

William Dana Chritchenson Jr. posed for this picture in his sailor suit. He later became the head teller at the Washington Trust Company. (GHU)

A local character poses for photographer F.W. Stiles.

Ben, Henry, and Mary Starr Utter in 1898. (GHU)

This group seems rather inattentive while waiting for the photographer to finish so that they can continue with their party with Henry Utter in February 1898. (GHU)

Grace Brown Abbott (left) and a friend share an umbrella on Weekapaugh Beach in 1898. Note the photographer's shadow on Grace's apron and the *McClures* magazine. (GHU)

A family poses while out for a carriage ride in the early 1900s. (GHU)

Fred Lena's baby is shown here in a wonderful bassinet. This photograph was taken *c.* 1910. (WS)

Posing on the porch and steps are three
girls and a boy, c. 1905. Note the fans
held by the girls on the steps. (GHU)

A lovely young girl poses in a very
ornate wicker chair. (GHU)

Elsie Rose, the sister of Weaver William "Quaker Billy" Rose. She is shown holding samples of his work on her lap. (WPL)

Anabel Austin, Dorcas Austin, Henry Austin, and Deacon John Austin sit with Elizabeth Austin and kitten. Dorcas is frowning because she didn't want her picture taken. (GHU)

This family portrait includes Mr. and Mrs. Edwin Pierce with Louise and Sam, c. 1936. (GHU)

John Delevan (?) was a famous storyteller in 1895. (Stiles)

Relaxing at home is George B. Utter II at 40 Grove Avenue in 1937. (GHU)

Three

School Days

The Elm Street School in Westerly, from a postcard marked 1913.

Babcock Junior High stands almost alone in this 1931 photograph.

A view of the new high school in Westerly, which was torn down in 1939.

A group of children
outside the
Pendleton School
on March 22, 1897.
(GHU)

In this photograph, a group of schoolchildren gathered tightly together to accommodate the photographer.

Seen on the steps of the Elm Street School are, from left to right: Ellen Pascoe, unknown, Alice Bliven, Bessie Segar, Gertrude Currie (?), Hattie Cross, L. Maxson, Edith Card, Nora Lewis, Mary Pendleton, Mabel Stillman, Maria Stillman, Alice Foster, Katie Sweeney, Jennie Stillman, Emma Dobson, Robert Robinson, Ralph Collings, Frank Woods, Stanley Lewis, Otis Chapman, Walter Way, Joseph Doney (?), Frank N., Willie B., Bertie M., Alex B., Nellie B., Henry D., Ruth M., and Sadie M. (WPL)

This group was all dressed up in special costumes for a play. (WS)

The Westerly High School football team of 1894 pose in a very relaxed fashion in front of the Elm Street School. (ENB)

Coach Dwight Rogers (in the back row) seems to be overseeing the Westerly High School football team of 1918 in this team photograph. (WS)

A school chum peeks out of the door as the Westerly High School baseball team pose for a picture. Note the center player, who seems to be sitting on the shoulders of the player in the front row. (WS)

The Westerly High School track team pose with their coach, who is kneeling at the rear right of this photograph. (WS)

Four

Patriotism

This postcard, marked February 1909, shows the Armory.

The White Rock Excelsior Club of 1867, with Ethan Wilcox, Reverend Albert Greene, Loranna Smith, Reb. Benjamin A. Greene, Hiram Arnold (grandfather of Annie Edmond), Mrs. Ruben Lamphear, Mr. McCleman, Mrs. Stephen Greene, and Dwight Smith (brother of Loranna), noted among others. (WPL)

This view of the Babcock Cemetery on Watch Hill Road shows a group of headstones, including those of Paul Babcock Esq. (who died on April 24, 1845, at the age of eighty-five years and twenty-two days), Samuel Babcock (who died March 23, 1813, at the age of eighty-two), and his wife, Mrs. Mary Babcock (who died May 1, 1822, at age of eighty-five). (WPL)

Robert Bonner poses next to the stone cut from the Bonner quarry for William McKinley, the twenty-fifth president of the United States (1897–1901). This is a c. 1910 photograph. (Bonner)

Civil War veterans pose in front of the Westerly Library, which is very appropriate, since the library was built in 1894 as a Civil War memorial. (GHU)

Crowds of well-wishers look on as the men in this photograph prepare to leave for the Spanish-American War in 1898. (WS)

This photograph was taken in front of the patriotically-decorated Girven establishment, which was built in 1908. The motorcycle is dressed for a Homecoming Days parade after World War I. Note the advertising for the Samuel Girven & Co. (WS)

The International Trust Company is shown here being dedicated, c. 1913. The inscription above door reads: "Built with Westerly Granite by Westerly Labor." (Bonner)

Written on the matte of this photograph is: "Civil War Veterans (?) 1925, Westerly, R.I. Left to right — Fred Holdredge, ___Knight, Charles Holdredge, Charles Stebbins, Samuel Tefft, Albert Chapman, Richard J. Rooney, Robert Knight." These men are shown with two Civil War cannons. (WPL)

A U.S. Army Red Cross wagon from Ft. Mansfield passes by a house in Watch Hill.

Five

Businesses:
Young and Old

A horse and carriage wait for their driver outside Willard Hardware in Westerly. (GHU)

Car No. 4, an open-type trolley, has many people sitting on board, with others on the side. The photograph was taken in 1894. (WPL)

Ed Maxson, town crier, is ready for duty with a notice poster. (Stiles)

This photograph of the Larkin Shore House in Watch Hill shows guests enjoying a "one-man band." (WPL)

These cows were brought to the Hoxsie estate to serve up fresh milk. (ENB)

The Smith Granite Works used oxen to pull wagons such as the ones shown here. The building was noted to be built in 1873. (Hoxsie)

This vintage oil wagon seems to await a fill up at the oil tank on the left. (WS)

This store banner reads: "Thomas J. Bannon [is successor to] Walter Price & Co. Wholesale [and] Retail Druggists." (WS)

Horace Vose shows one of his turkeys on November 20, 1886. He was famous for sending turkeys to the presidents of the United States each year. (Stiles)

Lamb's Fish Market and the town hall on Union Street as it appeared in the early 1900s.

This photograph is of the Cyclone Engine Company No. 2 on Union Street. S.M. Sharpe is the first man from the right in the front row. (WPL)

The Silk and Solway Mills on Main Street. This postcard is marked April 1907.

This postcard shows the post office in Westerly at a time when autos, horses, and buggies shared the roadways.

These people may be heading back to Westerly from the Clark Thread Mill in Pawcatuck.

Strollers hustle along the sidewalk in front of the David K. Hoxsie Dodge Plymouth sign in the 1930s.

These photographs are views of the David K. Hoxsie Dodge Plymouth garage, where the men would make parts unavailable to buy. This garage stood behind a church and the Hoxsie Accessory Store, where the Washington Trust Company parking garage is today. (Hoxsie)

The Hoxsie Accessory Store in Dixon Square on Broad Street. (Hoxsie)

A view of the Matheson Garage in the early 1900s, believed to be located in Watch Hill. (Hoxsie)

Several men pose for a picture near a Mobile Oil gas pump in the 1920s. Frank Mills (second from the left) drove the Mobil gas truck. (Hoxsie)

Trees line Canal Street in this view of the A.J. Myrick Grocery Store before the street was widened.

A photograph of Pucci's Radio Shop, with a pump of some kind, on the corner of Canal Street.

This photograph seems to be of the spot where Pucci's Radio Shop was on Canal Street. A truck has drawn up to the pump. Note the poster in the shop window; it states that the Ringling Brothers Circus is coming to town on June 11.

Six

Photo Gallery

A view of the Smith Granite Works. (Hoxsie)

This side view of the Smith Granite Works shows men working down in the pit and along granite ledges. This was the site of the first quarry, created c. 1840. The quarry's blue/white granite had the finest texture in the world. Mr. Smith, the founder of the Smith Granite Works,

brought in Italian stone cutters from northern Italy because of their quality workmanship. (Hoxsie)

Smith Granite workers pause for a photograph *c.* 1905–10, where Hoxsie Buick garage is currently located. This building was the last Smith Granite Works building standing. (Bonner)

This photograph shows the equestrian statue of George Washington at the Smith Granite Works. On the back of the photograph is written: "Taken from Rudolph Donato collection. Cut about 50 years ago in Smith Granite Co. of Westerly, R.I. and at the time it was the first and only equestrian statue in the world cut wholly from granite. Erected in Alleghany Park, Alleghany City, Pa. The figure was modeled by Edward Pauch, and cut by the late Zerbarine brothers Angelo and Columbus who were noted for their fine carving and sculpture work." (WPL)

Large blocks of granite await workmen in this photograph taken at the Smith Granite Quarry in Westerly. The whole yard seems to be at rest, in anticipation of the work to be done.

A c. 1870 photograph of the Smith Granite Works, showing the long shed which was connected to current Hoxsie Buick garage until the 1938 hurricane. (Hoxsie)

The water works at White Rock was very important to the townspeople.

Workers observe the workings of the water works at White Rock.

This mill appears to be located in the middle of the Pawcatuck River.

One workman seems to pause at the site of the Bradford Pumping Station. This photograph was taken August 24, 1937.

Workers and equipment are highlighted in this photograph of the Bradford Pumping Station construction in September 1937.

The Bradford Water Tower dwarfs a nearby tree in stature.

Two gentlemen leave their carriage long enough to observe the surveying for the Westerly Water Tower.

Surveying equipment takes the center stage at the spot designated for the Westerly Water Tower.

The scaffolding looks strained under the workers in this photograph of the construction of the Westerly Water Tower.

A man shows the extent of the trench excavation.

Notice the man standing to the left of the new Westerly Water Tower. The plaque on tower reads: "Town of Westerly, R. I. — Erected A.D. 1910 — Louis W. Arnold -Tristam D. Babcock — John (?) Carney — Board of Water Commission -Thomas McKenzie, Engineer & Supt. — Samuel M. Gray, Consulting Engineer — The Aberthaw Construction Company Contractors."

The workman in the foreground of this picture is ankle deep in water as he and others do trench work at Spring Street during drainage excavation.

These men are examining the ledge condition at the Spring Street intersection.

Oak Street with WPA workers in action.

This very old steam shovel seems to rest from its labors for this photograph.

This old piece of equipment is shown at Friendship and High Streets in 1919.

Workers concentrate on a new sewer line on Canal Street in 1919.

Seven

Street Scenes

Homes on Cross Street looking west from Chester Avenue.

These homes are reflected in street water in this view looking west from the King property.

The coupe seems to be seeking higher, dryer ground during road construction in this view looking east of the King property.

A lovely tree-lined street emerges following road construction east of the King property.

A photograph of the Lamb residence with its inviting open front porch.

A view looking west on George Street.

A view of the Ferraro property.

These homes are seen looking west from Granite Street.

The Anderson property and a neighboring home on Wells Street.

This intersection highlights homes on Greenman Avenue and Greenman Heights.

This serene view could be seen while looking south from the H.C. Perry property on Margin Street.

An automobile breaks the serenity in this photograph, taken while looking south from the H.C. Perry property on Margin Street.

Stately trees tower on each side of the street in this view looking north at the Thomas Perry property.

A gentleman is strolling past the Clancy property on Summer Street.

A car advances down Summer Street.

A woman strolling up the walk of a summer-dressed home. This photograph was taken before the widening of Canal Street.

The same summer-dressed home, shown here after the widening of Canal Street, seems ready for cool temperatures.

Oak Street hill before the 1935 WPA (Workman's Project Administration) work was complete.

Oak Street hill after the 1935 WPA work was complete.

In January 1936, WPA workers on Narragansett Avenue were working in 15 degree temperatures.

This car appears to be struggling along Boom Bridge Road before the widening project of January 1936.

Work has begun on Woody Hill Road near Bradford.

A car approaches on Noyes Hill Road before the WPA widening project of January 1936.

The Spring Street extension as it appeared in mid-1930s.

Two vintage automobiles rest on High Street at the entrance to Wilcox Park in the mid-1930s.

A view of High Street after it received a new pebble-looking surface.

Cars parked along High Street, which in the 1930s sported new sidewalks.

Peacefulness seems to surround this lovely home with its shaded porch and vine-covered arbor on Oak Street in the 1930s.

Shadows produced by some stately trees fall across this ornate barn and nearby home.

Work is about to commence at the site of the J.W. Berry residence on Newton Avenue on July 23, 1921. It looks to be a carefree summer day as clothes dry on neighboring lines and a flag blows in the breeze.

A woman walks toward two homes at the intersection of Newton and Wicklund Avenues in 1921.

An ornate streetlamp takes center stage in this 1931 photograph, which also shows several homes and a school in the distance.

This view of Elm Street in the early 1900s shows a telegraph bar in the tree on the left. (WS)

A serene spot in rural Westerly. (WS)

A fine team, wagon, and driver wait in front of 47 and 49 Elm Street. (GHU)

Written on the back of this photograph is: "Post Road — Westerly — House of Rev. Joseph Park built 1754. Post Road, Westerly near where Shore Road joins Post Road. Photo taken 1898. From Elisha Stillman Estate." (WPL)

The Gavitt homestead (aka the "Whipping Post House") with a carriage in foreground. The tree is still standing with leaves. This home was also known as the "Old Meeting House," because people gathered here during colonial days. The Whipping Post was where persons who went against the law received lashes for their misdeeds, such as stealing turkeys or sheep. (WPL)

The small boy in this postcard view of Elm Street was obviously aware of the photographer.

Union Street was a rough road to travel in the 1930s, as can be seen in this photograph. Note the Christ Episcopal Church steeple at the top of the hill.

A young boy sits on the curb in this rural-looking photograph of Dixon Street in Westerly.

This house on Larkin Road in Watch Hill was originally a farm cottage and horse barn at another location. It was moved to this site in 1895 (?) by Daniel C. Babcock. A third floor was added and it became rental property owned by his widow, Mrs. D.C. Babcock, until 1938, when it was taken over by their daughter and son-in-law, Mr. and Mrs. Robert E. Loomis. They ran it as a summer boarding house until 1965. It burned to the ground in 1969 (?) under another owner. This photograph was taken around 1940. (Courtland R. Loomis, Mr. D.C. Babcock's grandson)

Eight

Riverside to Ocean Shore

This *c.* 1900 photograph of Avondale on the Pawcatuck River shows the D.C. Babcock property, with the J.O. Babcock property beyond. The house is now owned by R.A. Booth.

The steamboat *Mystic* is flanked by its shadow in this photograph. The people aboard appear to be enjoying the ride on the Pawcatuck River. (WPL)

The steamer *Sadie* is shown here heading down the Pawcatuck River in the vicinity of C.B. Cottrell's. On the back of photograph is written: "Sadie 1884–1887. 105' in length . . . Donor Mrs. L.A. Joslin, Date about 1885–6." (WPL)

Harvey C. Perry donated this August 7, 1891 photograph of the *Schr. John W. Binnell*, a four-masted schooner, in full sail. A note on the information card states: "Deciphering of surname of the schooner may be incorrect." (WPL)

This serene photograph of Bay Street in Watch Hill is believed to have been taken at the turn of the century.

This postcard view, believed to have been taken around 1900, shows the Life Saving Station at Watch Hill.

This turn-of-the-century photograph shows the crew and Life Saving Station at Watch Hill.

The Larkin House in Watch Hill was removed in 1906.

Watch Hill Dock, Watch Hill, R. I

Sail boats rest at the Watch Hill dock.

This postcard, posted in August 1906, shows the Watch Hill Light of Watch Hill.

Several people can be seen on board the steamer *Watch Hill*, on a postcard marked August 1914.

This postcard, marked September 1916, shows the steamer *Block Island* landing at Watch Hill.

The merry-go-round at Atlantic Beach in Pleasant View (now Misquamicut), Rhode Island, from a postcard marked August 1917.

A view of Niantic Avenue in Watch Hill.

Aquidneck Avenue in Watch Hill, in a postcard view thought to have been taken in the 1910s.

These fans are watching a baseball game in front of the Ocean House in Watch Hill.

Several auto commuters arrive at the Ocean House at Watch Hill.

The Louis J. Powers residence of Watch Hill, from a postcard posted in 1933. This house was moved by barge from Springfield, Massachusetts, in the 1910s and was completely rebuilt in the 1960s.

This photograph, taken from a steamboat at the end of the Block Island dock, shows the Atlantic House. On the back of the photograph is written: "Watch Hill, given to library by Mrs. Robert Loomis, 1953." (WPL)

This Watch Hill cottage has a stone work gazebo and tower. The house is a gambrel-roofed wooden shingle structure. (WPL)

The Plimpton House in Watch Hill was opened in 1865. It is shown here with a large group on the lower floor and a smaller group on the second floor of the piazza. (WPL)

The Plimpton House and the old Watch Hill Post Office can be seen in this 1932 photograph.

Anchored sailing vessels and a steam tug boat (right) in the Watch Hill harbor. (WPL)

These bathers in Watch Hill are believed to be posing behind the old bathing pavilion. Note the fashionable bathing wear of the day. (WPL)

View on Ocean Avenue, showing Mastuxet and Ninigret Lodges, Watch Hill, R. I.

This postcard, marked November 1913, shows Ocean Avenue, including the Mastuxet and Ninigret Lodges in Watch Hill.

A postcard of Fort Mansfield at Watch Hill. The person sending this card in 1908 wrote on the back: "Hungry, waiting for dinner."

Moore's dock is shown here in 1936 along the beach on Fort Road in Watch Hill.

A view of Fort Road, Watch Hill, in 1936.

Several people pause to look at the view from this bridge in May 1936.

People stand on the bridge support for a view as a pedestrian approaches.

Traveling along the causeway in Weekapaug in 1934.

This wall was built to widen the causeway in Weekapaug in 1934.

The Weekapaug bridge was structurally damaged by the hurricane of September 21, 1938.

Acknowledgments

I gratefully acknowledge and applaud the advice and guidance I received while compiling this book. Photographs were acquired from the Westerly Public Library in conjunction with the Westerly Historical Society, from the *Westerly Sun* and the Burdick Collection, as well as from the George H. Utter collection and book *Old Pictures of Westerly*. Quarry photographs and information were donated by Donald Bonner, Issac Smith, and Ray Hoxsie. Many photographs were donated by individuals, including Laurence Rathbun. A very generous contribution of information and photographs was made by Courtland Loomis.

Legend

ENB — Edward N. Burdick collection
GHU — George H. Utter collection
Stiles — Frederick W. Stiles collection
WPL — Westerly Public Library collection
WS — *Westerly Sun* collection

Visit us at
arcadiapublishing.com

Printed in the USA
CPSIA information can be obtained
at www.ICGtesting.com
LVHW071026211223
766685LV00056B/929